FOREPLAY

THE ENTIRE POINT OF SEX

ERIKA MOORE

Table of Contents

Introduction

Foreplay can be the most amazing aspect of sex in the event that you get inventive. Infiltration is extraordinary and all, yet foreplay is the thing that gets you energized for the headliner in any case. All things considered, it's a wide term for the tempting, lively exercises that individuals participate in before sex. Moreso, keeping in mind that it's regularly acknowledged that foreplay ought to occur before intercourse, the inquiries of whether it occurs, how long it commonly endures, and how to zest it up and how to dominate foreplay are another story. There are inventive activities in bed, and many have nothing to do with what numerous couples consider "the headliner" (which means, penetrative sex).

There is no time limit, you can make it totally obliged your own insight, and it expects you to think outside about the crate. In case you're hoping to flavor things up in the room this time and attempt new things, the primary spot to begin with will be with your foreplay partner.

Chapter One

Foreplay Initiators:

Watch each other uncover

With sex, we regularly go on autopilot, and we neglect to take in each second, particularly in the event that you've been together for quite a while. All things being equal make a note to really observe each other uncover. Try not to contact one another while it's occurring either; make everything about the experience of taking a gander at one another and getting energized exactly at the prospect of how hot you both are.

Speak profanely

Rather than really contacting one another, essentially mention to one another what you need to do. Try not to be reluctant to really expound! To make it extra attractive, don't stand by until you're in the room. Essentially discussing all the messy, attractive, insane things you need to do to one another while you're perched on the love seat keeps things fun and coquettish.

Tune in to music

In the event that you don't as of now turn up your speakers while you're engaging in sexual relations, presently may be an ideal opportunity to begin. Whatever sort of music turns you both on, regardless of whether it's R&B, country, moderate tunes, or even show adjusts turn it and utilize the music as the mood of the entirety of your moves. Dance around the kitchen and chime in. Having a good time together is attractive! Making a playlist together of your main tunes to get down with.

Play with ice

It's totally free and has benefits for the two partners. It's an alternate and interesting sensation to play with temperature during sex. A few thoughts for adding ice into your foreplay remembers for your mouth during kissing, in your mouth during oral sex, scouring it down your partners body, or on you or your partners areolas. In the event that ice is a lot for you and you wouldn't fret getting somewhat untidy, dribbling frozen yogurt down your partners body (or yours!) can get the job done (and it tastes cracking great!). Be cautious about utilizing any food sources close to the vagina in the penis to evade diseases.

Head off to some places that help you to remember your relationship

Return to your first date, where you got ready for marriage, where you said "I love you" interestingly, and that's only the tip of the iceberg. Being in those unique places again can bring you back, intellectually and actually, to prior pieces of your relationship. It'll remind you how far you've come as a team … and if that isn't only somewhat hot to you, I don't have the foggiest idea what is.

Make a can list together

Plunking down together to think of all that you need to do this year explicitly is the ideal foreplay for the audacious couple. The things can be as insane or as agreeable as you need them. Keep this rundown where you can return to it, for example, your end table, and make it an objective to do something new consistently.

Send a book

In spite of the fact that our telephones can make us somewhat less present for sex, they can likewise be an extraordinary device to stir the two partners. Text your partner precisely what you need to do to them when they return home — and simply like the messy talking exercise, don't be excessively terrified of subtleties. You can send it toward the beginning of the day or not long before you realize they're going to come over. They'll be on their way right away! Different thoughts incorporate messaging your partner that you need to have intercourse (basic, however viable!), about your number one sexual involvement in them, or something you're eager to attempt. In case you're both 18 and more seasoned, sending photographs in your number one undergarments can be a great method to flaunt precisely the thing they're returning home to

Wash up together

While your partners in the shower, don't hesitate to jump in! Shower sex doesn't need to be the ultimate objective of this all things considered. Having some good times in the water and getting energized for anything that's to occur outside of the shower is energizing all in itself. Nonetheless, we're not against attempting to make shower sex work — simply don't hurt yourself!

Chapter Two

Foreplay Tips That Lead to More readily Sex

Try not to deal with foreplay like a fast pre-sex necessity.

On the off chance that you put in a couple of quick minutes on foreplay, racing through like it's a plate of crude vegetables to snack on before the substantial fundamental course is served, your partner will not simply feel cheated—they'll have the option to tell you're not into it, which is a charisma executioner.

Extend your meaning of what foreplay implies.

Foreplay occurs in each snapshot of association that happens among you and your partner, from the second you awaken. Anything that impacts our psyches can possibly affect our sexual coexistence.

While they may not appear to be associated, assisting your collaborate with clothing or offering to do the dishes might be the most accommodating thing you can do to clear a path for closeness," she says. "Anything that takes something off your partner's plate, and supports their overall feeling of unwinding, goes far when it comes time for sex.

Tell her the amount you need her.

Offering your sexual partner genuine praises will tell you the amount you appreciate her, and that may cause her to feel hotter before your garments even hit the floor. Master proposes "revealing to her the amount you want her," and how lovely she is. Realizing that you would simply prefer not to have intercourse, you need to have intercourse with her is a turn-on for some ladies.

Tell them you need them as soon you stroll in the entryway by praising the manner in which they look: 'You're considerably more blazing around evening time than when I left earlier today. Request what kind from foreplay she loves, and you'll learn something.

You can generally improve as a sweetheart, yet you're not a telepath. Notwithstanding focusing on what she reacts to, asking is the most ideal approach to realize what gets her into her.

The main key to being amazing at foreplay is correspondence. Numerous partners expect that all ladies are turned on by contact, or direct sexual play, however few out of every odd ladies would list that as their best option.

Assist her with preparing loose and to play.

Following an unpleasant day brimming with commitments to other people (work, kids, family, and so on), getting personal might be the farthest thing from her brain. Help her move into an alternate headspace with a *pressure-free* decompression meeting.

Breathwork Exercise

Breathwork is characterized as "cognizant, controlled breathing done particularly for unwinding, reflection, or restorative purposes." It can help your partner (and you, in case you're down to attempt) to reconnect with her body in the midst of life's stressors and interruptions.

It may sound odd to do breathwork as foreplay, yet I have instructed around many ladies how to utilize it as an approach to get energized for sex. It incredibly successful in light of the fact that it removes them from their reasoning, controlling, judging, and arranging brain, and places them into their inclination, associating and detecting mind—which is the way to astounding sex for most ladies."

Soft talk sweet stuffs into one another's ear.

Possibly (non-filthy) talk sounds not exactly suggestive to you, however it can carry you and your partner nearer with amazing outcomes. "Feeling personally associated can be the hottest foreplay for certain ladies, when ladies genuinely share their cravings, their feelings of dread and what they love about their partners. Many couples have revealed to me this is the best foreplay they have at any point attempted."

Kissing

Recall the first run through you two kissed? On the off chance that you do, you realize that kisses are a definitive science test, and probably the snappiest approaches to associate with your sex partner.

A straight forward yet serious makeout meeting. "Kiss with energy as you press your whole body against theirs. Permit yourself to truly feel the full-body contact, focusing on the pressing factor, surfaces, temperature, and forms of your bodies." Utilize your mouth on her (not simply in the manner in which you think).

Drifting your mouth this near her skin will construct expectation, Also, take a stab at licking her in a touchy spot and breathing warm air over the smooth way you've made. Work your way down around the sides of their bosoms. Bother over their areolas and underneath their bosoms. S-l-o-o-o-w is the key here—except if she requests that you accelerate, and take as much time as is needed as you drop down to between her legs, "proceeding to utilize breath kisses to attract attention to each square crawl of their body.

Become acquainted with her with the rear of your hand.

Utilize the backs of your hands to back off and construct excitement. Try not to want to get, manipulate or apply pressure immediately. All things being equal use plume light touch.

Massage her thigh.

Utilize your fingers, palms, tongue, toys and lips to crawl, lick and kiss all around their internal thighs without making a plunge between their legs, Float your mouth over their lips and clit to construct want, and make them throb for additional."

Attempt "the Pussy Pocket."

This technique is not very intricate, but at the same time it's tied in with going slowly—so how about we separate it into steps:

1. Place your palm on the pubic hill and crease each of the five fingers over the vulva (that is all the sweet stuff outwardly).
2. Press against their vaginal lips to make some warmth.
3. Rub gradually and delicately from the outset, and afterward increase the speed and pressing factor by following the beat of their hips
4. Pulse your full hand against them, or undulate in a wave-like movement to shift the sensations.

"The W" is another approach to utilize your hand. Press your level open palm over their vaginal lips, the long way. At that point, "Open your fingers to frame a W (or a V), and slide here and there as you open and close your fingers. Use loads of lube so you can slide around and increment the pressing factor as their excitement constructs."

Contact every last trace of her body to advance full-body climaxes.

Beginning at their head, work your way down the rear of their body, changing the strokes, pressing factor, dampness and development across the whole surface of their skin. Whenever you've contacted every last trace of their rear, turn them over and kiss, contact, touch, and lick from head to toe on the opposite side prior to jumping down between their legs.

Regardless of whether she doesn't have an awe-inspiring peak subsequently (and great sex isn't characterized by accomplishing one), she'll walk—or ecstatically roll—away inclination flushed and loved.

Furthermore, you can fan the blazes by not contacting.

In the first place, set a five-minute clock. At that point, advise your partner they are not permitted to contact you back until it goes off. Then, utilize your mouth and hands to kiss and prod your way around their erogenous zones, without remaining in one spot for a really long time.

Blindfolding

Blindfolding your partner—in the event that they appear into the thought, obviously! — To increase their different faculties. "At that point, substitute utilizing your lips, tongue, fingers, or a toy on various pieces of their body," she says. You can make the play a stride further with a sexy game, in which they think about which part or item is contacting their body.

Change things up to keep things new.

After years in a relationship, it's not difficult to fall into a trench—and examination recommends that trying new exercises can help revive your enthusiasm. Leather expert proposes exploring different avenues regarding when and where you get provocative, as well.

Present assortment by changing the setting in which you start foreplay, in the event that you regularly stand by until you're sleeping at night, attempt some morning foreplay in the kitchen.

Chapter Three

Sweet Stuff/Word as Foreplay

On the off chance that sweet things can bring you endless snapshots of joy, what's the damage in being considerably more insightful and discovering what energizes your partner.

Expressing certain things that can cause your partner to feel better and perform better in bed is a simple method to accomplishing sexual joy. Notwithstanding, causing your partner to feel spoiled doesn't mean you continue making glossed over comments about their room execution. Rather center around things that they would really very much want to hear from you. Besides, these comments need not be fundamentally ignoble yet a slight sexual tendency is an additional preferred position, as it will allow your partner to perform better each time you get personal.

Relationship master states, "Offering sexual comments to your partner gives them a kick that causes them to feel reveled and upgrades their certainty levels as well. In any case, it is vital to understand what your partner likes to hear in bed. Additionally, guarantee that you say the perfect thing at the perfect time, as it will impart a sensation of having a place. Telling your partner that you like his/her moves in bed can add to their sexual ability."

Things that energize ladies may appear to be radically unique from what stirs men, however the truth of the matter is the two partners like being lauded for their sexual moves. While for men, it's a greater amount of appreciation for their sexual exhibition, for ladies it's the spoiling and sweet commendations that hold the way to delight. Recall not to say anything at the last minute or only for it as it influences your sexual relationship over the long haul.

A specialist on sexual relations clarifies, "While in bed, appreciate your partners non-actual characteristics, their actual credits, things that they have accomplished for you, their sexual activities and so forth It's an issue of selecting the correct things. Try not to lie since things said in scramble are not valued throughout some undefined time frame as they were not legit assessments."

Chapter Four

What Men and Women Love To Hear In Bed

What Ladies Love To Hear In Bed

You are as hot as could be expected: Ladies love improving approach to compliment her than with interesting commendations about her body and sex advance. Calling her hot, excessively provocative, energetic will cause her to feel exceptional. Ladies love to be viewed as extraordinary and diverse without fail, so as opposed to contrasting her presentation and the last time, disclose to her how astonishing she is each time you enjoy a sexual demonstration.

I love playing with your body bends: Quit depicting yourself as a wild creature standing by to jump over your partner; stay quiet and let your demeanors do the talking. Try not to allow your lady to feel that you need her just during peaking minutes, rather show that you similarly appreciate foreplay acts like playing with her body. Since ladies don't care for ungainly commendations about their bodies, so proceed cautiously.

Try not to go over the edge remarking on a female's genitals as it might cause them to feel like you consider her to be a sex object. Praise her figure, skin, and afterward proceed onward to more explicit remarks.

Your groaning makes me insane: Once more, a commendation, yet this time totally sex situated. Despite the fact that most ladies would avoid advising you in the event that they had an ideal climax, they would unquestionably adore on the off chance that you reveal to her how her groaning sounds bring you into a fit. "Most men like a noisy lady in bed, as it informs them as to whether they're giving you enough joy or not. By revealing to her that you make the most of her groaning, you guarantee her that she's going the correct way to excite you for more activity,

You play an ideal temptress: This should be an authentic commendation and your woman love will very much want to hear this. Revealing to her how consummately she has dominated the craft of enchantment will take her to incandescently happy. Also, she would gadget some more up to date intends to excite you the following time.

Select segments where a female partner has been offbeat in the sexual demonstration and has accomplished something which you generally needed and enlighten them regarding this. Such an expression would help her solace level and give her a criticism that you like her temptation methods,

I appreciate kissing each inch of you: Sounds excessively basic, however exceptionally compelling! Tell your ladies the amount you love her body and an offer of kissing can be the most ideal way out. Truth be told, ladies are more joyful during foreplay when contrasted with bad-to-the-bone sex moves in bed.

Ladies love to be spoiled and kissing her is extraordinary compared to other excitement acts. It's ameliorating to hear that you love her whole body and she thusly would be more requesting in her sexual joy,

What Men Love To Hear In Bed

We should make it a memorable night: It is ordinarily accepted that men are more sex driven and need to appreciate each night consequences be damned. Yet, in the event that a female partner shows an equivalent degree of interest in the lovemaking act, it can do ponders. Your man would cherish it on the off chance that you shed all hindrances and appreciate the evening of energy more than ever.

Such adorable articulations initiate a degree of certainty and men get a guarantee that it's not just him who's intrigued to engage in sexual relations on a specific evening, however the female partner is similarly included. It additionally gets a sensation of being needed and men love that.

I love it when you contact my pressing factor focuses: While directing your man to your groan zones is a certain something, yet telling him that he's right in his moves is seriously invigorating. Uplifting statements can tell your man that you are getting a charge out of the thing he's doing. Whatever you do to hail them will make your sex frolic really energizing, so don't stop for a second. Discussing the sexual demonstration itself and giving a legitimate input helps an extraordinary arrangement. Appreciating how your partner has dealt with you in bed and sharing how well it felt is something incredible that men love to hear.

Dear, how about we have a go at something new today: Recall, neither a man needs to play a failure in bed nor he wishes to have intercourse to a repetitive partner. In this way, be a lady magnet and told him that you also love testing in bed. Disclose to him that you're quick to make a special effort.

Men need to give shot fresher positions and love making acts. Indeed, men love a partaking partner in bed, so whatever point they see a female showing a drive, they get mixed.

I love when you get more stunning: It's alright to get grimy and wild now and again, however the thing matters most is telling your man that you're OK with the sexual style. Men frequently expect a female partner doesn't care for getting too wild in bed, however while appreciating the joy minutes, in the event that you give indicates that his wild demonstrations are turning you on, it tends to be a second to keep an eye out for.

Through such signs, the man won't just feel excited, however will feel better. Likewise, he would be astounded to see a wild side of yours, so he'll put forth more noteworthy attempts to cherish you the manner in which you need,

You realize I generally fantasized about this: Adulation consistently works and if it's tied in with sharing your most out of control dreams, nothing better than that! Ladies, by and large, are famous to share their sexual fixations; however a man would adore it if his female partner is straightforward in bed.

Men love being direct and they like impending partners in bed, so offering your dreams to your darling can be a tremendous turn-on and they would absolutely very much want to hear it,